A BOOKWORM
WHO HATCHED

by
Verna Aardema

photographs by
Dede Smith

 Richard C. Owen Publishers, Inc.
Katonah, New York

Meet the Author titles

Verna Aardema *A Bookworm Who Hatched*
Jean Fritz *Surprising Myself*
Lee Bennett Hopkins *The Writing Bug*
Rafe Martin *A Storyteller's Story*
Cynthia Rylant *Best Wishes*
Jane Yolen *A Letter from Phoenix Farm*

Text copyright © 1992 by Verna Aardema
Photographs copyright © 1992 by Dede Smith

Richard C. Owen Publishers, Inc.
P.O. Box 585
Katonah, New York 10536

Library of Congress Cataloging-in-Publication Data

Aardema , Verna .
    A bookworm who hatched / by Verna Aardema : photographs by Dede
Smith .
        p .   cm . — (Meet the author)
    Summary: Noted children's author and storyteller Verna Aardema
recounts her life and describes how her daily activities and writing
process are interwoven .
    ISBN 1-878450-39-5 (hard)
    1 . Aardema , Verna — Biography — Juvenile literature . 2 . Authors ,
American — 20th century — Biography — Juvenile literature .
3 . Authorship — Juvenile literature .   [1 . Aardema , Verna .
2 . Authors , American .]   I . Smith , Dede , ill . II . Title .
III . Series : Meet the author (Katonah , N. Y.)
PS3551 . A56Z464   1992
813 ' . 54 — dc20
[B]   93-12002

The text type was set in Caslon 540.
Editor-in-Chief Janice Boland
Production Manager Amy J. Haggblom

Printed in the United States of America

9 8 7 6 5 4 3

To my sister Melva Johnson,
the youngest of the Norbergs

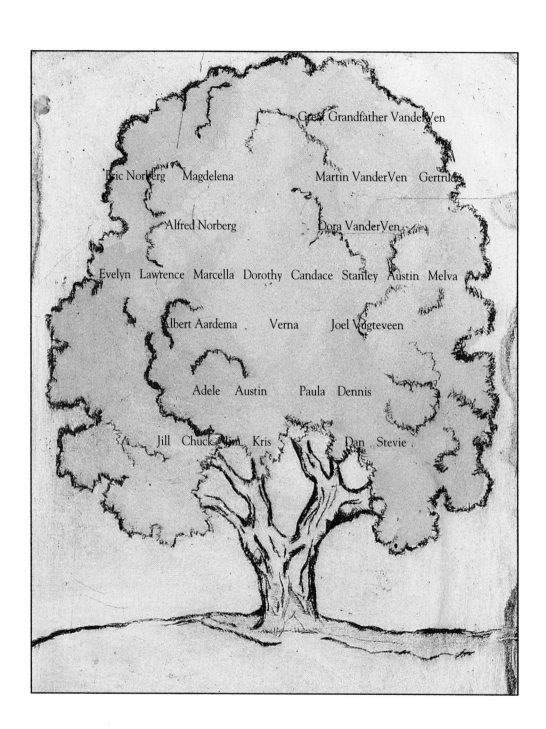

I am a reteller of folktales.
I was born on June 6, 1911
in this house in New Era, Michigan.
My father built it in 1903 for his bride.
The house was the family home for nine children,
for Papa until he died in 1956,
and for Mama until her death in 1973.

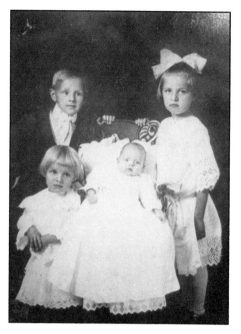

When I was a baby, a traveling photographer
took my picture.
The apple was supposed to get me
to look toward the camera.
The next year, a traveling man
photographed the first four children:
Lawrence, 4, Evelyn, 6, me, 2, and Baby Sally.
After this, either no photographer
ever came to our door or our mother
was too busy to let one in.
The five children who came later
were sorry about that.

For me, becoming a writer
probably began with loving stories.
Mama read to us children as we sprawled on the floor
around her rocking chair—me near the back
so I could hide with my tears if the story was sad.
My first very own book
was *Hans Andersen's Fairy Tales*.
In my small rocking chair at bedtime,
I would read "The Little Mermaid."
After finishing the story in tears
because of the sad ending
I'd crawl into bed with my little sister Sally.

We children loved to act out stories.
Mama let us play with her wedding dress.
It was the inspiration for many a show
which we and our friends put on
upstairs in the carriage house.
It was all we needed to create
a folklore princess or a Sleeping Beauty.

A cedar swamp back of our homes
was my and my cousin Elaine's special domain.
In it we explored patches
of wild flowers and squawberries.
We climbed trees to peep into robins' nests.
And we visited our *secret room*.
That was a cave-like space inside a clump of trees.
It was carpeted with black swamp soil
and our furniture was a fallen log.

One day, when I was an eleven-year-old,
"nose-in-the-book" bookworm,
Mama read a poem I had written
and she said, "Why, Verna,
you're going to be a writer
just like my Grandpa VanderVen."
At once I decided to make writing my career.
After that, to escape having to help with the dishes
I would run off to the swamp.
Alone in my dark *secret room*
I would sit and think and think
until I thought my sisters
must be finished with the dishes.
That's when I made up my first stories.
Soon, I began writing down the stories
I thought of in the swamp
and asking God to help me to become a good writer.

In high school I wrote school news for the paper.
At Michigan State College
I took all of the writing courses.
I began my writing career as a staff correspondent
for *The Muskegon Chronicle.*

My first husband, Albert Aardema,
was as happy as I to see
"By Verna Aardema" at the top of a story.

Our little daughter, Paula,
got me started writing for children.
I had to make up stories to get her to eat.
I mailed a "feeding story" about Africa to a publisher.
The editor suggested that I use it
as chapter one of a juvenile novel.
I did African folktales instead.
And *Tales from the Story Hat* was born.

The bookworm I was had hatched.

I was an author!

I have published more than 25 books.

Because I retell folktales,
I have to start with an authentic tale.
One day a college student
from Nigeria, West Africa, came to our house.
He told us a traditional tale his grandmother
had told him when he was a child.

I usually find the tales I retell
in old books, obtained for me
through interlibrary loan.
By computer, librarian Ann Fields
locates and requests the source book I ask for.
She uses codes for the title and for the author.

After finding a folktale I like
and deciding how I want to redo it
(tell it in my own words),
I write it first in pencil.
Then, using the typewriter,
I revise it at least three times.

Then it goes to my agent
and she forwards it to the editor.
If the editor buys the story
she helps me to perfect it. Then the type is set.
The many corrections on this galley proof
show what happened when by mistake,
the first version instead of the final revision
was sent to the typesetter.

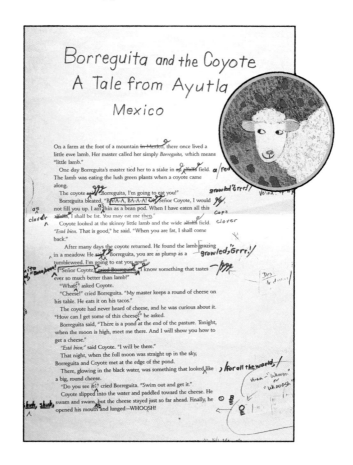

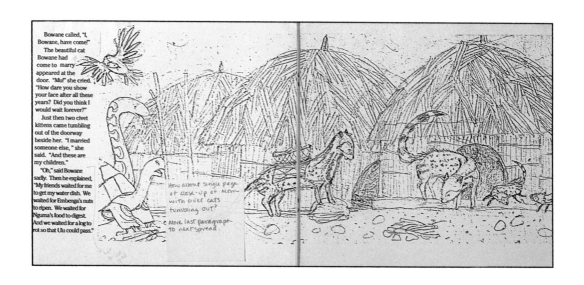

Next, an illustrator is chosen to do the pictures.
The illustrator cannot *tell*
the editor what he plans to do.
He has to *show* her!
So he makes book dummies.
This is one which Will Hillenbrand made
for my *Traveling to Tondo*.
He made it of paper and cardboard.

WILL HILLENBRAND
808 LEXINGTON AVENUE TERRACE PARK OHIO 45174
513-831-5830

Dear Verna,

Thanks for including the dummy ~~foo~~ from Traveling To Tondo, in your forthcoming book A Bookworm Who Hatched. I'll look forward to seeing the book after it comes off press.

Tell Joel I said <u>Hi</u>, I hope the both of you are well.

All Best,
Will Hillenbrand

Will says, "I think in pictures."
On a letter to me
he drew what he saw in his mind
for a bookworm who hatched.

20

Finally, the story goes to the printer.
Eventually, the day comes when the book
which began as a code on the OCLC
(Online Computer Library Center) computer
comes off the press and my advance copies arrive!

My first husband Al had died in 1974,
and the next year I married Joel Vugteveen,
who had grown up with me in New Era.
In 1984 we moved to southwestern Florida
to be near my son, Austin.

Early mornings are cool and lovely here.
Often I'm out picking up the paper
before the stars have dimmed.
I read the news and do the Jumble puzzle
while I eat my breakfast.
Joel and I like to swim and
to bicycle around the park.

When our children and grandchildren come to visit,
I often bake a pie for dessert.
Making a tasty pie is as important
as writing a good story, I think,
and you can't *eat* a story!

Stevie is my youngest grandchild.
He likes to stay at our house
for a few days at a time.
He is a bookworm, too.
When I take him shopping
he spends his money on books.

Being an author involves more
than just writing the books.
For me, it also means speaking and telling stories
in schools, colleges, and libraries.
It's a busy life.

On days when I have a lot to do
I often get up from the table after eating a meal
and go straight to my office.
Joel calls that "going to the swamp,"
for, just as my sisters did long ago,
he has to do the dishes all by himself.

At the end of the day I watch TV,
usually a baseball game, with a book on my lap.
If the book is very interesting
Joel watches the game for me,
and I only look up at the exciting parts.

Writing is not easy but the rewards are great!
When starry-eyed boys and girls
tell me they want to be authors,
I hug them for success.
One of them later wrote to me,
"When I become an author and visit schools,
I'll tell them that you hugged me
and I owe it all to you."

Other Books by Verna Aardema

Anansi Finds a Fool; *Borreguita and the Coyote*; *Bringing the Rain to Kapiti Plain*; *Oh, Kojo! How Could You!*; *Why Mosquitoes Buzz in People's Ears.*

About the Photographer

Dede Smith lives in north Florida. She is an award-winning freelance photographer. Her interests include art photography and exercising, and she is a Macintosh computer enthusiast.

Acknowledgments

Photographs on pages 5, 6, 8, 11, and 14 courtesy of Verna Aardema. Art on page 13 from *Oh, Kojo! How Could You!* by Verna Aardema, illustrated by Marc Brown. Copyright © 1984 by Verna Aardema for text. Copyright © 1984 by Marc Brown for illustrations. Book in photograph on page 21 is *Anansi Finds a Fool* by Verna Aardema, pictures by Bryna Waldman. Copyright © 1992 by Verna Aardema for text. Copyright © 1992 by Bryna Waldman for pictures. Used by permission of Dial Books for Young Readers, a division of Penguin Books USA Inc. Corrected galley on page 17 from *Borreguita and the Coyote* appears courtesy of Curtis Brown, Ltd. Art on page 17 from *Borreguita and the Coyote* by Verna Aardema, illustrated by Petra Mathers. Illustrations copyright © 1991 by Petra Mathers. Art on page 19 from *Traveling to Tondo: A Tale of the Nkundo of Zaire*, retold by Verna Aardema, illustrated by Will Hillenbrand. Illustrations copyright © 1991 by Will Hillenbrand. Reprinted by permission of Alfred A. Knopf, Inc. Photographs on pages 18 and 20 appear courtesy of Will Hillenbrand.